When Life Breaks

WHEN life BREAKS

Raising Children During Divorce

TANZANIA DAVIS-BLACK

NEW YORK

LONDON • NASHVILLE • MELBOURNE • VANCOUVER

When Life Breaks

Raising Children During Divorce

Published in New York, New York, by Morgan James Publishing in partnership with Difference Press. Morgan James is a trademark of Morgan James, LLC. www.MorganJamesPublishing.com

ISBN 9781642795011 paperback
ISBN 9781642795028 eBook
ISBN 9781642795424 audio
Library of Congress Control Number: 2019902189

Cover and Interior Design by:
Chris Treccani
www.3dogcreative.net

Illustation by:
freepik.com

Morgan James is a proud partner of Habitat for Humanity Peninsula and Greater Williamsburg. Partners in building since 2006.

Get involved today! Visit
MorganJamesPublishing.com/giving-back

For Joshua and Jaylen.
Thank you for giving me the
most precious gift of all: Agape Love.

TABLE OF CONTENTS

INTRODUCTION

When an individual experiences heartbreak, a financial break, or a mental break, it is manageable. However, when children are involved, it becomes extremely difficult. It becomes depressing to manage a break because of the windshield crack effect. When it is divorce, the fractures permeate relentlessly and they will inevitably reach the children.

No one who gets married for love plans for a divorce, nor should they. The idea is that when you take those sacred vows you have entered into an infinite life-binding contract. It is expected of both people who pledge themselves until death to fulfill the promise. This is, in part, why divorce is so difficult. Because even in situations where divorce is the best course of action for both people it is not really something anyone anticipated having to do. Many of us entering divorce are blindsided and unprepared for what divorce entails. This lack of preparation is only exacerbated by the information that is readily available. The majority of the information is legal and does not seem to account for the fact that the life we share with someone else is about more than assets or other aspects that can be easily divided by lawyers or the court system. What this means is that very few people have a clue as to what to expect or how to navigate the minefield of divorce when children are involved.

When facing the reality of divorce, life has changed. Life as we knew it has broken. How do we deal with that when it comes to the children? As you read this book and as you experience the divorce process firsthand with a child or children, the one thing I want you to remember is that the decision to divorce someone, regardless of the reason why, is a decision that is deeply, inherently an emotional one. Ending a marriage is deciding to end a part of life, the part that was connected to one's identity as a married person. I consider children to be the greatest asset created during the marriage. They are the sum of the two people who are deciding to divide. And sadly enough, the children have no voice, no decision-making part in the process. They become innocent bystanders, often screaming but unheard. Because the divorce process is so emotional with multiple moving parts, I liken it to a roller coaster.

There are a lot of certainties in life you could name—yes, we will die, and we must pay taxes, etc.—but there are two certainties that I have become most acquainted with which are true from the moment we take our first breath until the moment we take our last breath. The first is that life will change on you—there is nothing constant but change. The second is that life will break. Life comes with this unspoken warning, everyone knows it as there are thousands of quotes about it. It comes with this warning label: "Fragile, handle with care." We know the fragility of life, we hear it in eulogies—gone too soon. We get it. We all inherently know that life has its breaking moments. And it is lessons like that, it's those inevitable encounters in life that I want to shield my children from because I don't want to see them hurt. But when you encounter divorce…. Hello! The break has already occurred. They will experience it when there is a fracture in the home. When there is a fracture between two people that make up that child's whole they are now broken. So we find ourselves standing in the midst of a trying question: How do you deal with that break?

Very vividly I recall standing in line for a roller coaster water ride. I, like any parent, want to protect my children. I want to shield them from the cracks and breaks that are going to occur in life. On that roller coaster, while we were standing there, I assured my youngest son that it was ok. We took five flights of stairs up to wait our turn. He was terrified. Through his labored breathing he asked, "Mom are there any sudden drops?" Then he said, "I changed my mind, I don't want to do this." Instantly my thoughts negated the option of walking back down. Not after we just made it up five flights of stairs and I had yet to catch my breath from the walk up. No, I was not prepared to just undo this. So I prayed that I was not a liar … or at best I could use this as a teachable moment.

I threw out this random, half-witted rationale while standing in line: There are five people on a raft and we are just holding onto straps, we aren't going to be buckled in, so they can't possibly do a sudden drop and besides you'll be sitting next to me. Don't worry, I've got you. We got on the ride, we had some screams, there were no sudden drops. It was fine and dandy. "Let's do it again," he shouted. We repeated that ride three times in a row. So then we had this next ride called the Tornado. I don't know how I missed the details of the ride on the sign, but I am certain it said nothing about a sudden drop. Nonetheless, we proceeded to that line. I assured my son again. No problem, you're fine. This raft holds four people and like the other we are holding onto straps, and we are not going to be buckled in and I am quite sure they are not going to do a sudden drop with four people just holding on to a strap. Trust me, this is going to also be fun. He, myself and my niece were in the raft. When we pushed off we noticed the lights escorting our raft into the tunnel. My son bellowed out pleased with hearing his echo, "How cool. I like the lights." My niece sounded off, "This isn't so bad." Before I could agree, I spotted something that made me a liar. I didn't see something that I needed to see. I did not see a bottom. Oh…No…where is the bottom. Panicked thoughts invaded my mind on this joy ride. I looked at my son, instantly I became frightened. I had lied. I was searching his face for forgiveness. I can't save him from this. I want to but I can't and I am sorry I lied.

There was a life lesson in that moment which became the principle for my divorce: that communication is imperative and you must speak the truth. I didn't know there was a sudden drop and I should have prepared him that there could be a sudden drop. I should have done my due diligence and just asked someone. I, on the other hand, had given him the assurance that everything would be ok. We do this in so many ways, verbal and nonverbal. We act as if we can shield our children from everything bad by not saying what needs to be said. But we can't. It is something vital I learned and applied during my divorce. I have to communicate with my children. I have to listen to them, and I have to speak truth to them. And when I find myself placed in circumstances that are testing and challenging me, I must keep my composure for their survival.

Well, at this point, we started to pick up the pace. My niece looked at my face as her back was facing the drop. She caught that bolt of fear that shot through me and landed on my face. There was nothing I could do. It didn't matter how many degrees I had. It didn't matter what the bank account looked like, how old I was, or how much wisdom I had accumulated over the years. I could not save him from what was about to happen. I saw it and wondered would he jump, would he let go of the very thing that was sustaining his safety in our raft. Would he trust me to hold on.

Much like in life there was about to be a break. I wanted to know how would he handle this unexpected break. We were about to fall, things were about to fall apart there. And I was scared, not for me, although I don't like the sudden drops, but my fear was for him. I didn't know how he would be impacted by this and I wanted to save him from this unwanted experience but there was nothing I could do. Much like life, we can't undo this. There is no option, the break ... the fall is coming. Now you have to brace yourself. What do I brace myself with? The answer is with whatever strength you got. The straps of life.

That fall was coming so fast and I didn't have time to get a lesson out to prepare him.

What do we do during the fallout of a divorce and with the children are on that raft with us? I have already stated that communication is utmost. But before we start communicating, so that we don't give broken, ignorant, untruthful advice, we have to make sure that we the parents are whole first.

Every divorce is different. Factors such as why it's happening, who initiated it, and how quick the process plays out, all have a pivotal role in how you feel or how much time you require to process what is going on. Based on that there is no single thing that is going to help you through this trying time in your life. There is no amount of provisions that can be offered to fully prepare you for being a co-parent or single parent. Parenting will test your emotions, your stamina, your nerves and even your sanity. While you are dealing with divorce and navigating the single parent lifestyle, stepping into both the role of father and mother to your children, you will find it a major challenge trying to be an amazing parent.

However, this book may serve as a tool to help you navigate through some of the obstacles you will face while trying to raise children. While the book can be read from cover to cover, there are times when it may be beneficial for you to take a non-linear approach. I invite you to take such an approach as a means of coping with specific situations as they arise in your life.

The first chapters of this book deal with common challenges that are faced when undertaking the option of divorce with children involved.

Subsequent chapters focus on dealing with the emotional aspects experienced. When children are most affected by this decision, it is not uncommon for them to shut down and shut out those around them. Trying to communicate with children during such an emotional time is like pulling teeth. But they do need to release. They do need to be heard. Each section is directly related to something I have felt or experienced. This section will be most helpful if you are in the beginning stages of a divorce, or if you have a divorce which is ongoing.

Having journeyed through this process, I understand that despite all efforts, all best attempts, the pitfalls are still there to catch us off guard. I leave remedies to such encounters that aid in navigating around or over if not solving them.

My Story

It's four a.m. and I find myself blinded by the darkness of the hotel room. My nearest relative is at least two hours away. The solitude, the silence, and the darkness begin to suffocate me, as panic and anxiety seep in. I can't breathe because I am alone and I have never been alone … like this. I'm trying to breathe, trying to think, struggling to comprehend what just went down. But moreover, I'm craving feeling something normal. My emotions are crashing about so erratically with a speed so violent. And though the emotions are twisting about me, I feel a mental state of paralysis.

It is all a blur. The hours that whipped past midnight where a dramatic tug-of-war with my spouse over something so petty–at least to me–led to me exiting my own home in the dead of winter without the protection of winter gear. Instead, I am blanketed with fear, confusion, hurt, and solitude that would constrict my mind as I sit there trying to figure out what next.

I had just been thrust into the first stage of divorce, the separation phase. In this moment I am alone without anyone who can identify where I am physically, spiritually nor emotionally. I was afraid that I was so numb because I know firsthand what happens when pain breaks through.

I treat pain every day. As a dentist, I watch how infirmities sit quietly inside a tooth, brewing while often times ignored. I know all too well that temporary fixes and medicating a problem will come to a head and the restoration of these things can be costly.

This was not a dental procedure that I could navigate through smoothly, although I had been here before. This was my second divorce. The familiarity of the process you would think would allow for some peace of mind. It wasn't that simple. My first divorce was much different. I had no assets, no children, no shared accounts, not even a home. I just had a two-bedroom apartment. I was choking on fear in that hotel room because as straight forward as my first divorce should have been, it gripped me emotionally. It ripped at my faith, my confidence, my sense of security, and left me financially at square one. The remembrance of the physical and psychological state I stood in with that first divorce shook me to my core because I would have to cross that same bridge with a much different twist. Gripping me were the assets that we created and knowing they could not be divided easily in this second divorce. For how do you divide children? I had no experience in such manner as I grew up in a two-parent home as did most of my childhood friends. And for the few who were of single parent homes, there was no talk of separation or divorce, the single parent home was a pre-existing reality before they were born. I feared the worst for my sons. I had witnessed from the advantage of growing up in a two-parent household how life still meets you head on with challenges. The curiosity would not escape me of how a divided home would affect my sons' lives. Furthermore, my sons were not teenagers with a deeper understanding of life. They were still in toddler and preschool phases. At this knowledge, I wrestled with fear of the unknown and an unpreparedness of how to educate them on divorce and what the next chapter(s) of their life would be like. Advice from many concerned loved ones would pour in, which added acid to my open wounds of fear, insecurity, and doubt. The erection of such daunting emotions would occur because many of the people offering advice or critique had never sat in the state of darkness I was in. I appreciated the support but to abate the anxiety, frustrations and panic I would need to search in the depths of my being on how I would manage to cross this bridge of divorce again but with my children by my side. You see, at this moment the very first step in separation was the hardest and filled with agony for I had never spent one day since my sons were brought into this world without them sleeping next to me. Now a dark reality was upon me which I was not prepared for. I would sleep this first night without my babies.

Of all the assets I had accumulated over the ten years of my marriage, I would have relinquished them freely. I would, without the slightest hesitation, have parted with the multiple rental properties acquired, the home which was my very first home I purchased, the vacation property, and yes even my dental practice if it meant I could spare my children from the byproducts of divorce.

In my eyes, divorce was imminent. It has been my experience through studying and living life that sometimes you have to amputate a part of something to save something. It is a difficult decision. No one wants to lose any part of themselves. But when a piece of you has decayed, it must be removed to spare what is healthy.

The initial detachment in divorce with separation is the most difficult. There is the awkward adjustment phase. Our life, our emotions, unfortunately don't come with an owner's manual. I could have used one. I had to learn how to enter such a place of isolation, fight through the legalities while armored with next to nothing, and simultaneously shield my children from those terrifying statistics that lurked in every corner of my mind.

I once read an alarming statement that "the death of a parent is less devastating to a child than divorce." The article I read ended with that statement. The author of the article carefully led up to such a painstaking statement with multiple statistics, many of which I had heard before. The fact mentioned that fifty-percent of marriages end in divorce was no surprise. But the statistics regarding the emotional peril that children of divorce earn lower grades than their peers and are less pleasant to be around (Andrew J. Cherlin, "Marriage, Divorce, Remarriage") was alarmingly new to me. As a mother of two boys, I could not close the article with short-term memory regarding the statistic that "Children of divorce, especially boys, tend to be more aggressive toward others than those children whose parents did not divorce. (Emery, Marriage, Divorce and Children's Adjustment, 1988). But above all thirty plus statistics I would read, the most alarming was the one from the Journal of the American Academy of Child and Adolescent Psychiatry People that stated that people who come from broken homes are almost twice as likely to attempt suicide than those who do not come from broken homes. (Velez-Cohen, "Suicidal Behavior and Ideation in a Community Sample of Children")

How would divorce affect my sons? What role would I need to step into in order to place my children on a path other than what statistics forecasted? Their home would be sold and it was the only home they knew. I would have to come to accept the nature of the custody arrangement and what it meant to share. How I would construct a bridge between two homes to make it seamless for my three- and six-year-old evaded my minimally creative mind. What truth do I speak to them about what lies ahead? I would come face-to-face with the effects of divorce and how I would have to dig deep internally. It would mean searching within myself for strength, patience.

My heaviest challenge at times would be controlling my emotions in such a manner that they would not violate my senses and ability to maintain sensibility. The emotions would represent the straps on that raft. Out of fear, anger, frustration I would find myself just wanting to let go. Emotions would rage inside of me in a way that I wanted to break out and just scream. But my ex was already screaming in ways through the courts I had never witnessed before. Someone has to be quiet to hear, especially hear the children. The children have to be seen and not forgotten that they matter most in this process. The children have to be felt. They are going to ache and overflow with their own set of unique emotions and I would have to be prepared for the break and the leaks of those emotions. Would they act out at school? Would they become withdrawn, depressed? Were those statistics a forecast of what would happen to my children? These are the questions I struggled with and still hold close as

I continue to raise them to this very day. Statistics about school dropouts, drug addiction, depression hang about my children like a noose magnetized to their necks simply because they are products of a divorce.

And the greatest hurdle of all was how to communicate effectively with someone who now stood opposed to me in every way. His back would be upon me. He had deafened his ears to anything I would have to say even if it were in his favor. The crevices that ran through us were deep now that we were separated. Even worse, our children existed about these cracks dangerously. I needed him as he needed me for their survival. I feared that the divorce statistics about children meant nothing to him. It was a problem and I knew there was a solution. I just had to unlock the code.

I spent three nights in that hotel room trying to figure it out quickly. As I prayed to God for a listening ear and for wisdom, I was preparing a strategy.

Those three nights would pale in comparison to the next three years. This legal roller coaster of divorce would drop me, throw me, thrash me, and often times leave me in such a way I felt lost.

I was fortunate that in those darkest pockets of my life, I was not alone. My faith accompanied me with the help of others who offered sound advice and a listening heart. Still, I would have to figure out ninety-five percent of this journey on my own. Sometimes I would speak with someone who was curious about my divorce and its cruel process. The conversation would inevitably end with the person saying, "I don't know how you do it. I would have ended up under the jail. I could not have made it if I were you." But I did make it. I remembered the emergency brake when the roller coaster became unbearable and unending.

The emergency brake was simple. I just had to locate it. I knew he had been my best friend before the marriage existed. I trusted that although the divorce process transformed my one-time close friend into a someone who was unrecognizable, that friend who I once trusted and pledged a lifetime to still existed. It would take patience. It would take much prayer and, most of all, understanding to find the one person I needed most to help me raise my children effectively. I would need that friend, that confidant, the other half to show up. I figured it out that just as emotions ripped through me, they raged and roared within him as well. I would be able to detach without angst because I would sit with my own emotions–grief, fear, judgement, anger, tension, etc. and acknowledge them, study them so I would empathize with what he was feeling. Then I could interpret this foreign language that spat from him verbally and nonverbally. The language that evolves over time from when you first meet and when you're in love is much different and very foreign when you're going through a divorce. We use outside people such as family members and attorneys to interpret that language for us instead of realizing we already know it.

A great orator once said, the lessons we learn are only ours for the moment we are going through them. They are meant to be honed and fashioned in such a precise manner to be used as an instrument by someone else. I share my story because it is out of gratitude that I found my way to the other side from marriage to divorce with my children thriving, communicating, living, and loving. I owe God and the universe for the favor I received in finding a treasure so valuable which could have been easily destroyed. I co-parent effectively with my ex. While I lost so many assets, I still have my practice and my ex-husband, my best friend still manages the office with me. My ex-husband and I found ourselves on that roller coaster ride of three years through darkness and back and survived the bumps, the falls, the breaks. Which meant the world to my children as they express it so clearly today.

As I write this book, I'm reminded of my favorite flowering plant, the orchid. I had several orchids and could not figure out how to keep them alive. I would do everything right, they only needed a weekly drop of water and sunlight. Seemed simple, but they would die after a few months and I would reluctantly toss them and purchase another. They aren't cheap, by the way. I would let go, give up and start again. Then one day, someone received an orchid as a gift and I expressed my love for the plant. Just as I was about to explain how difficult the care is to sustain their life, someone interjected just in time to offer up a lasting solution. She said, "Be patient, the leaves will fall, the beauty in them will fade, but it is not dead." I was grateful because I thought that the last orchid I purchased was yet again dying. I thought about the former orchids I had tossed. But because someone shared a piece of experience from their life with what I was struggling with, I now have a beautiful orchid that, through patience, I have watched the petals fall and through nurturing the new buds have blossomed.

If one crumb of information is granted that could help someone keep her sanity, her willpower during the darkest moment, then I believe that information is worth being shared.

FACING THE CHALLENGES

Divorce and separation create an acute sense of loss. The person you came home to each day, confided in, and with whom you created a life routine is now absent. This absence, physically and emotionally, is a tremendous void for you. With children involved, you have lost your partner with whom you shared the day-to-day joys, responsibilities and challenges of parenting. Each person deals with loss uniquely. Many people expect that dealing with the feelings of loss from a divorce is something they can "work through" or "get over." However, for most, the reality of coping with a significant loss is that it is both a chaotic and cyclical process with good days and bad days.

It can be presented that while we are going through a divorce, whether we acknowledge it or not, we're also going through the five stages of grief. There are an array of emotions that come into existence for all involved during the divorce process. The stages of grief, in short, involve experiences with denial, anger, bargaining, depression, and acceptance. The weight of this life transition is difficult to address within ourselves, and the gravity of knowing the children are transitioning with these very same emotions is equally, if not more challenging to address.

"Volcanic" is the one word that comes to mind as I remember going through this character-building moment of my life. I call it character-building because it was just that. Yes, most definitely it was a difficult, and tortuous time. Nonetheless, it tested every fabric of me. The inner core is like a volcano, sometimes dormant and then out of nowhere it is as if every emotion has become the fiery contents of lava which are stirring inside ready to erupt. Just when you would like to take a selfish moment and nurse those afflictions there are the children feeling the same quandary of emotions as you.

The children sit in a stupor of emotions doused with confusion and burdened with many questions.

A colleague asked me in the middle of a discussion about a patient's case, "How did you do it? How do you accept being served divorce papers at the office and still work with the very person, running an office and co-parenting? Is there some secret practice you do? Is it some form of meditation? I want to know because I would have lost my mind." My response was simple: M.O.T.I.V.A.T.I.O.N. Without M.O.T.I.V.A.T.I.O.N. yes indeed, the three pressing years of a legal battle would have been the emotional, mental and psychological death of me. Imagine my fate without M.O.T.I.V.A.T.I.O.N., being in and out of courts, hundreds of interrogative questions, disputes over custody, split households, school age children with different set of needs, and the financial obligations, along with operating a dental practice right alongside of the very person who is punching at me on the sidelines Without a single doubt. A family member said to me, "You know this was supposed to be the knock out, the TKO, in your life, but miraculously you are still standing. You have just lost almost everything." I responded, not my children, I still have them and I still have an obligation to see them through this. They were my motivation, a lifeline for myself in order to raise them in the fashion they demanded and to thrive.

I turned each letter of the word motivation into a step that allowed me to put one foot in front of the other to keep moving. Often times, it is difficult to be there for others when you are finding your own way. But, unfortunately, I did not have such luxury of choosing self only as I did with my first divorce. I would find them just as wounded, spinning in just as much misery as myself.

The method applied to helping my children was:

M - A Mother's Love

This is the easiest of all. It costs nothing but yet is so inherently powerful in aiding the children through such a difficult time. Children's behaviors are naturally expected to change, and most often in unpleasant ways. Perhaps it is a question that is asked, or simply relaying personal business from one household to another that will create friction. Just showing them love and letting them know you are there for them is worth more than you can imagine.

O - Open Mind and Heart

Understand that this is a trying time for your children as it is for yourself and there is no owner's manual on how to transition through a divorce as every divorce is unique. Have an open mind and heart that the children have allegiances to both parents but find themselves between a rock and a hard place. My sons explained to me that the divorce was so difficult because they did not know whose side to take. The children love both parents and at times they need something more from one parent than the other. Keep an open mind that when they desire to see a parent or spend a little more time with a specific parent they are not choosing one over the other. It is a tug-of-war inside of them so be patient.

T - Table Talk

A very effective tool. Sharing a meal and conversation allows for the ease of discussion. It facilitates a means of understanding where your children are on the emotional scale, how they are coping with the losses and new-found way of life.

Talking however does not have to be limited to meal time. It could be a car ride to school or just to the grocery store, talking in a calming manner when doing a leisure activity provides a comfortable setting for the child to express themselves.

I - Ideas with Creativity

This is a dismal time. The joy has been stripped from their lives as they are introduced to and bounced from one residence to another. Tensions can often run high for the co-parents but with an open mind the creativity can flow. Because of all the changes occurring, and it will vary from day to day, your creativity and ability to solve challenges with a creative spontaneity will be invaluable. How to handle two sets of rules, to merge seamlessly, is a struggle aside from all the other challenges. The notion that one house might be more "fun" than the other puts pressure on the parents as they are merely just trying to help the children cope. Being prepared for such comparisons between houses will take a bit of creativity on your behalf. You may not have every electronic device the other parent has, nonetheless there are hundreds of other fun projects that can be offered up to the child which will be just as fun and rewarding.

V - Veracity

Simple, very simple. You have to be truthful, honest. Indeed, truth hurts but also helps with children developing a high state of resilience. This is critical in healing. Tough questions arise. In the beginning it feels as if a new question, a different expectation for the answers arise every day. A tactical but honest approach is best. Oftentimes, it will take the alliance of the coparent so that an appropriate answer will be given. One frequent question centers around why the divorce took place. Children are naturally inquisitive and want to know why their lives were turned upside-down. They also want the assurance that it is not because of them. Being truthful allows them to see that the divorce is directly related to the parents although the consequence of divorce affects them.

A - Assign Responsibility Appropriately

Often when things fall apart we look for something or someone to blame. The tensions created make it easy to be judgmental and point fingers, often pulling the children in the middle. We adults set the bar for our children and must be careful about how we place blame, careful not to bash the co-parent in front of the children. But moreover, if we ourselves have erred, we must be responsible enough to make amends and apologize quickly to diffuse the chaos.

We can find this useful, especially in speaking truth. Take ownership for what needs to be owned but by no means sit and ruminate over the past. Address it and move forward. If the fault lies within the other party, learn to forgive and demonstrate that for the children to see. They can only gain insight as to how to live healthily when others have erred.

T - Therapy

Don't be afraid of reaching out. Divorce with children is no easy undertaking. Receiving help from appropriate sources is a must to ensure the children are healthy mentally and emotionally. Therapy exists in so many forms. A counselor, a pastor, or even a trusted family member. Elders of the family are often amazing at offering the gift of hindsight. Reach out to a reputable resource and don't be afraid to say "Help." You and your children are not the only ones navigating this. There are many others and just knowing that someone has gone through these same obstacles with solutions eases the stress.

I - Intuition

You know your children best of all. However, as we are tending to our own emotions, legal issues, fitting all these new changes in with work and other daily activities, the connection with the children can easily be lost. Stay connected, stay in touch with them on various levels by checking in. Even when the dust settles, and the divorce is final, the emotions still linger. The questions still linger. Adaptation to the new has occurred but as you are still rebuilding your new life, new challenges will arise. It is easy to assume that once the divorce is final everyone should be ok. Just as in death, it is stated you must go through the four seasons before you feel some sense of restoration. The children will have continued questions and emotions that naturally develop through childhood, through adolescence, and into adulthood. They will be more exaggerated because of the divorce and activities they take on over the years. Still, stay in touch with what is happening is the greatest advice I can offer up. They will need you just as much then as in the beginning of the divorce.

O - Open Communication

Keep the flow of communication with the co-parent and children fluid. Don't shut doors because of how you are feeling at the moment. Keep in mind the children still have two parents they want to share their lives with. There will be birthday parties, graduations, award ceremonies and sometimes they want to reach out and just talk to the other parent. Keep that channel open. It can provide as a life line to the children. With today's technology it is far easier than before. Allow the co-parent to share in special events or even non-special events. Despite the fact that day to day roles have been altered to part-time with child custody orders, the obligation as a parent to our children is full-time.

N - New Life

After the dust settles, it is a new day, a new life. Perhaps new schools, new friends. I find it best to use each new encounter as an adventure and I have gained so many teachable moments through such novelties. As my sons are young and seeking my guidance, I collect each teachable moment, sharing them with my children as if they are precious gems. Knowing that one day I will no longer be in the parental position I hold now, they will rely upon these gems in adulthood. Everyone's role shifts from being a parent of a minor to being an adult's parent. I think back on the poems, the stories, the teachable moments my dad and mom offered me. They were utilized in moments I stood at a crossroad, not knowing what to do, they aided me in making sound decisions.

DETACH WITHOUT ANGST

Often when life does not meet our expectations, internal chaos begins resulting in an array of emotions:

Tension
Sadness
Anger
Confusion
Jealousy
Fear
Resentment
Concern
Manipulation
Judgement

Relief

If asked which of these I experienced during the divorce process, I would answer with a resounding all of the above. These emotions would come in waves and at times all at once stemming from the roots of pain. The shocking truth is that when checking in with my children they were also riddled with this same set of emotions. It was not just a matter of serving myself the ability to detach, I found it necessary to aid my children in the detachment process.

You may only experience a fraction of these emotions or find yourself experiencing conflicting emotions at the same time. At times you may find yourself in the thick of tension while your children are in a state of fear and panic. It is a conflict that must be delicately handled.

The arena of non-attachment has long been explored by Buddhists and the discovery has shown that attachment is the primary source for pain, with ego standing front and center. Non-attachment according to the Buddhists, is the theory that pain comes with an image of how we see ourselves in a complete or incomplete state. This image is tied into how we see ourselves in relation to our surroundings. For example, it is normal to feel a sense of security, happiness and fulfillment within a marriage. However, when it ends, that attachment is altered along with our view of ourselves, our happiness, and our fulfillment in life. If we feel this pain, then certainly the children are left with the same pain as their very existence was created because of the union between two people whom they depend on. They are born into attachment without any free will to decide their fate. They will be affected the most during the detachment phase.

The first two concepts employed through M.O.T.I.V.A.T.I.O.N. are relevant during this time of detaching as they help to make the transition a positive one. Motherly love above all must be employed, but with a careful design of mindfulness and observation with an open heart for understanding. It was best medicine of all for my children. The nourishing words I could offer up which just signified my presence would often mean more than I knew at the time.

Usually before the onset of divorce is the consultation with an attorney. This is the first step in detaching during the separation. I attended a consultation session with one attorney which lasted two hours. Just listening to all the legal terms and realities of what divorce would cost in terms of splitting and selling off assets and bargaining chips to be used as leverage evoked emotions I had been holding back. Near the end of the session, the attorney asked if I was ok because, without my permission, a tear trickled down my cheek. I was a bit embarrassed because in my mind this was to be a professional meeting. I had become overwhelmed and frankly lost in that moment.

I knew that the detachment would be part of the deal, but with so many scenarios poking at every emotion how would I be able to do this with a collected, composed posture. Especially if this was only the beginning. I was already leaking through the cracks. I would have to pull it together and find a useful resource that would allow me to detach accordingly without the angst so that I could smoothly transition my children through this process as best I could.

While giving all the love of a mother that I could, as I left that attorney's office, I realized that I would need to couple that love with mindfulness. A keen mindful intelligence is critical because it allows the mind and all its faculties to be in touch with what the body as a whole is experiencing. Mindfulness through meditation, communication, and an open mind, when involving children is a must.

I grew up in the Baptist church which made it easy for me to lean on faith in God as a source of peace. Expressing that faith with my children would be one vehicle for us to maneuver through this detachment process together. Being mindful and mastering it through faith allowed me to calmly maintain an open mind and to be the support my children needed. I wanted to abate the symptoms of the negative emotions. Being a novice at this, I started about it the wrong way. I offered pleasure as opposed to something practical and beneficial. It wasn't until my oldest son said something to me that jolted me with an "Ah Ha" moment. In my usual offering of ice cream, treats, and snacks, my son rejected my offer with a truth I knew but had ignored. He simply told me no, he did not want the night time snack because it was not healthy … even though it was just a slice of cheese. He further stated, that he did not need the cheese because it was late and it was not our family practice to eat late. He closed his reasoning for the rejection with, "We are only eating because we are hurting, but the late-night snack will just hurt us more later on." At that moment I knew I had to be open to listening. As the parent, my ego often had to take a backseat so that I could listen. To have enough love and mindful thinking would facilitate my openness to hear my children. I understood that this process would have to be done together.

Before I could impart any education to my children about pain and its process during detachment, I had to embrace inherent truths about pain. You cannot bargain with pain, you cannot run from pain forever. It is inevitable. I recognized that if I fight pain, it will snare me. On the other hand, if I embrace it too long with constant rumination, it will become my master. It is only through willful submission to its existence that pain and all its acquaintances (i.e., tension, confusion, envy, and anger) will dissipate.

In raising my children through this three-year ordeal, we found ourselves in a new stance, unified dealing with the detachment together and healthily.

I was open to trying something different. We were in the midst of what I called a valediction party. My youngest son suggested having the party but without the food. So at night when someone could not sleep, we would do a bedtime story and discuss how it made us feel or what our opinion was. We would even share our current emotions, staying connected to how we felt, asking questions for answers. A common question we would pass around would be "Does anybody feel like…?" My favorite was does anybody feel like shouting or crying. I would even start the party off with a deep question: Is anybody angry? Raise your hand and share what you are angry about. I wanted to hear the answer. I did not want to blind myself from what they were feeling. Even if it meant the answer was they were angry with me. I knew all too well what happens when you run from pain. If you run today and return tomorrow, pain is the unwanted guest that lingers and you'll find its presence greeting you when you return. With children I found it best to sit with those emotions, embrace them without guilt or shame and just have that valediction party together. We would just let all those emotions that make up the human existence be felt through acknowledgement. It was the best detachment remedy we experienced. When you do that, you inform pain and unwanted emotions that life will go on. It may take a day, a week or perhaps a month, but the presence of pain will fade and you will discover a stronger, more resilient you. So, my sons and I found ourselves transitioning through those moments of angst by sharing our fears, sadness, concerns, anger, and even releasing our tears together. The greatest challenge I discovered in confronting pain is that everyone has their own way of taking on that challenge. My sons and I had three different ways. Although I was battling my own way through pain, I found it necessary to find out their way of coping. My oldest son is the intellect, and being the oldest wears armor around his emotions. The walls are dense and I struggled with penetrating them. My youngest son has very few walls and is quite expressive, sometimes too much. I would have to help them through the pain and angst of the new life in their unique ways.

I invited my sons to express their pain through a painting or some kind of art so that we would be able to hold it. My youngest son without hesitation jumped at the chance to paint. We named the painting "the image of pain." The goal was to make pain tangible and visible to us all as it would sit on the breakfast counter. When we were done dealing with pain we would rip it up, part ways with it as we discarded it. My oldest thought the idea of painting was pointless. Besides, he steers clear of any artwork involving paint. I knew that he liked balloons. So, in the party store I asked him to point to the balloon he least liked. He selected a helium filled balloon that represented a haunted feeling. I purchased it and said that is what pain is like. I informed him that if you don't confront it, it will continue to haunt you. Therefore, we will use that as your symbol of pain that can be held and discarded when you are ready to release it. I personally chose to both do a painting and to select a balloon. I felt it necessary to show my sons that I identify with them in their own unique experience and expression of pain. It was important to show that no one's expression of pain was greater or lesser than the next. It was just different. When my time came to release, they witnessed my release.

It took months before we could release but it happened. We learned that pain is neither friend nor foe, it is simply a mediator connecting the experience with the life lesson. Submit to it, be compassionate to its nature, for it will free you.

COMMUNICATE
WITH CONFIDENCE

Communication is vital to existence. It is what sustains us as a culture. Communication is powerful, it can start wars or provide healing to masses. In undertaking the arduous task of raising my children during the divorce, I knew that how I communicated could help heal them, or cripple them by exposing them longer to suffering. I had already begun to exercise the main component of effective communication with mindfulness, compassion with understanding. I had formed a union with my children to navigate this difficult time, but now it was time to employ the next element: talking and listening.

Often when hearing the word communication, talking comes to mind. I found that even as the parent, I would have to spend even greater time listening. My sons and I found ourselves embracing the pain and the suffering of all the residual emotions. We held it in the compartments of our hearts, our minds, our souls. But just as I have witnessed up close and personal what happens when holding on to an infirmity, the same goes for toxic emotions. It is simply not enough to acknowledge the pain and suffering, it must be treated.

I saw a young man in my office one day on an emergency basis. Before I could enter the treatment room, I noticed an enormous swelling on his left cheek. As I stood before him, I noticed that the infection had spread to the lower eyelid. However, interestingly the infection source was from a lower tooth. I asked him when he first noticed the swelling. He responded that he woke up that morning like that. He stated that he was aware of the tooth ache for months but he self-medicated it and the pain began to subside and due to his fear of dentists he decided he would just wait. I explained to him that I would refer him immediately to the surgeon as it must be dealt with swiftly or it could cost him his life.

And so it is with communication. It is not enough to just be mindful and observe the pain, you must address the ailments around suffering with effective communication. As a mother, it was difficult to face the truth that my sons were angry—and partly at me—because of the divorce. I had to come to grips that their world was turned upside-down and I played a vital role. But, just acknowledging pain won't treat the disease. If it festers where it started, just as the patient's abscess, it will spread to other parts of the body. It will affect a child's sprit, self-confidence, self-esteem, and how they interact with the world.

Now I entered into a delicate realm of communication that sounds simple but is quite the opposite. I would soon discover that my children were evolving exponentially because of the divorce process. I no longer had the three- and seven-year-old I had before the separation. Their fast-paced evolution was taking place because they had to adapt. Adapting to survive. Compassion and understanding would take on a whole new meaning through a vessel of insight.

I would have to learn to bite my tongue, relinquish the urge to exercise my executive parental control, and listen. The need to relinquish my position and lend a listening ear– whether it was hearing my children or the co-parent–would be trying at times and tested me beyond measure. My absolution in doing so would be to heal the infirmity in my children. They were my motivation.

The greatest challenge I found was that veracity must exist in all that is communicated. For what good would the antibiotic do for the young man with a spreading abscess if it were the wrong choice? It is not enough to just talk, speak, listen–communicate without the healing component of truth. Being false to just temporarily abate the situation would be the same as nursing the abscess at home with an over the counter med or a neighbor's pharmacy prescription. The truth must be exercised but in a delicate manner specific to the child you are speaking with.

To kick-start most communication, I would engage in conversation at the table. I called it table talk with my children. Always with their selected meal and beverage at home where they feel most safe and comfortable, I would initiate a topic and then just listen.

It would be like lancing the infection. All the disease that was populating their bodies and minds would spill out and I would watch their relief as they exercised their autonomy to speak without judgement or punishment.

More often I was unprepared to handle some of the questions and would have to delay the response. And in truth I would communicate that. There was one question my son asked that I would need to take a step back to reflect on just how to answer. "Whose fault is it for the divorce?" Remember the game truth or dare? Well, as I managed to choke down half-masticated food, in that very moment I wished it were a dare that I could take on. Sometimes you just aren't ready to answer certain questions. If you aren't and you find yourself pinned at the table without any diversions for an escape, it is best to just state that you have to think on this a while so that you explain it correctly. Well, he persisted insisting that the answer was easy, he deducted that there are only two people in the marriage and there was an end. He was only three and wanted a simple answer.

It was at this moment I came to a huge understanding that when dealing with my then three-year-old toddler in such crisis, every form of communication would have to be handled carefully. For it is a grave challenge to skillfully understand what may be wrong with a toddler as their attitude is constantly changing. Bouts of emotional reactivity and regression were a constant battle with my youngest that had to be dealt with delicately. As a toddler, his level of understanding was minimal, leaving him little control over his emotions. I was concerned that the fears and distress would convert to resentment.

The behavior where a loss of developmental accomplishments is often referred to as regression. One aspect of regression, bedwetting, was experienced although he had been potty-trained for over a year. Emotional reactions played out in the preschool class room as he withdrew from participating or even following directions. These scenarios would test limits in me as I wrestled constantly with how to extract from my toddler ways to get him to communicate what he was feeling.

I tried my best to delay that conversation, and I could have exercised an executive power as the adult, as the mother to terminate such conversation. But, I had to call upon compassion through a state of mindfulness to treat this emotional infirmity that was growing in size right at the table. With empathy for his suffering, I set aside my irritation at the fact that I was being challenged by my child and so I committed to standing with him as a three-year-old companion. This would allow me to see that the question was not that difficult to answer at all. As an adult I was making the question harder than it really was. I just needed to sit with him in the moment. He simply wanted an answer, and I was in possession of what he needed. So, I answered him. Because I was listening, I heard him say that there are two people in the marriage and the marriage stopped. He wanted to know who stopped it, who was at fault. I calmly answered him with, "Because there are two people that make up the marriage it would then be both people who ended the marriage." "Son, it is both our faults...." I explained to him on a toddler level with an example. "If I asked you and your brother to watch a glass dish sitting on the table, and your brother began shaking the table causing the dish to fall and break who should we blame?" The three-year-old said, "My brother broke it. He would get the blame!" I explained how unfair that would be to put all the blame on his brother because both were in charge. And since he was in charge too, he could have simply removed the glass dish when he knew it was at risk for falling. Well the marriage was that dish and two people were in charge of it. It doesn't matter much placing blame on one person because it won't fix the break. But both are responsible.

By applying such tools of compassion and understanding, what often seems complicated becomes diminished to a far simpler state. It is not easy to perform these practices if we as parents are not connecting within ourselves first. We get in our own way blocking such progress in mindfulness as we are battling the process of divorce. Divorce can bring out the worst in both people. As in my case it was a war with multiple battles. But this is where the mindfulness through insight can be your greatest weapon.

In raising children during a divorce, we invariably have to deal with the co-parent. I found it to be neglectful in thinking any other way. I am only one half of my sons' makeup; their father is the other half. It would have been selfish of me to excommunicate him from our sons' lives. If I stood in each of my son's shoes, I would no more desire to be alienated from either one of my parents. Simply put, it would be unfair and deviant. Dealing with a co-parent who is gripped with a handful of emotions that you are not privy to makes it that much more of a challenge to provide your children with everything they need to heal. For me, it took all of the above: the faith, mindfulness, compassion, empathy, insight, and understanding to transcend the pain that my co-parent possessed.

It was morning time in the office and the day was moving about just smoothly. I was in the middle of reviewing a case with a staff member when another staff member summoned me to the side and stated an officer was there to see me but had instructed him to meet me in the break room. I was calm because I had not a clue as to what this could be about. The divorce had just begun, the gloves were on at this point. Well, I still had my mask on, but lowered it just below my lips to be audible when speaking. Soon, to my surprise, the officer's intent was to serve me divorce papers in the office which he did. I thanked the officer for his time and signed for the documents and went about my day as normal. When it was made known as to where I was served, friends and family alike were shocked. They were more shocked at my disposition of calmness than the fact that I was served at the office. The shock was merely because I was just served and still went about the day, the week, the months working with my co-parent, future ex-husband as usual.

"How do you do it?" someone asked me. I said it is not easy, but my children are the motivation to maintain my composure. In spite of whatever sorrow you are feeling inside as a result of your separation/ divorce, the desire to fight becomes secondary to the children. In that moment, while holding those divorce papers, I knew the manner in which I would go about this divorce. My attitude would affect my children and their future. I could not afford to make the divorce solely about me.

In order to re-establish solid communication with my co-parent, I would need the lines of communication to be repaired. The equipment to repair those frayed lines would be "all of the above" as outlined earlier. I would utilize the moments of shared custody to perfect my talents in mindfulness instead of viewing time away from my children as doom and gloom. When they spent time with their father, I would use those moments of solitude to meditate on occurrences throughout the divorce that would ignite fear, rage, envy, worry, pain. I would be led to a place of understanding that it would be selfish to think that only I felt angst about the break-up. It was his home too, his life that was also broken. His time would be divided with his children, his life would be altered in the worst of ways as well. I employed a compassionate heart for my husband who stood now in opposition to me, not just in court but in life. It was that understanding that allowed me to facilitate a dynamic line of communication with my ex-husband and a trust in God that if I established the right line of communication, we (my sons, my ex-husband, and I alike) would all be restored.

I now possessed the greatest weapon in this three-year war of divorce. Because of my pain and suffering I would be able to interpret my children's pain. I would recognize the foreigner who stood before me at my office and would be able to work with him despite the harshness and often vindictiveness behind the scenes that were shared on legal grounds. I found empathy and would use it in a resourceful manner.

Veracity rivals empathy in strength. The truth when spoken to children, and the manner in which we speak it, can be either healing or toxic. I try at all cost to be very mindful as to what deposits I make within my sons. Often times, in practice, I treat mothers who are still nursing. The mothers present for treatment which most often needs to be deferred to another time simply because the procedure will require anesthetic. I ask of them to express enough milk and store enough for a few days in order to avoid what was injected into their body being consumed by the infant. As parents, as mothers, we take all precautions to protect our innocent children. This should be particularly exercised when dealing with communication. The wrong kind of communication– if it's in haste, ill-tempered, or incorrect–can be detrimental to children during such a time of fragility.

HEALING
THROUGH THE PAIN

We have now discussed how to embrace pain with mindful awareness and compassion. It has opened up the gateway to this vessel of compassion and understanding which allows the communication channels to broaden. Not only are we able to hear but our awareness allows us to listen with a presence. We are able to leave our guarded posts to stand alongside the child or co-parent and empathize with their view point. As wonderful as the elements of embracing pain, mindful awareness, and compassion are for all involved with the divorce, it is not the total makeup for completion in healing.

When it comes to the healing process, I presume that I am no different than most. I become quite impatient and tend to rush the healing process. I witness this phenomenon on a constant basis in my practice. It is not a rarity to treat a patient with an infection so severe that the tooth requires for me to extract it. Accompanying the pain is the impetuous desire for instant healing to occur. This request for such haste in healing violates the biological and physiological order of life. It is impossible to remove a tooth, dislodging ligaments and passing a tooth through bone and gum tissue, and expect that complete healing to occur at the end of the appointment. And so it is with raising children through a divorce. It would be unfair, blatantly egregious to expect the children to be ok or simply get over it after being made aware that the parents are splitting up and living in separate households. On the other hand, it is not uncommon to feel that way.

There would be nail-biting moments such as when I felt that the thousandth time I had to console my preschooler because I would not be staying the night would be the last time. There are legal ramifications for spending the night during a period of separation.

After all, separation comes with the process of divorce. I would enter a moment of judgement thinking, why can't we all just get over it and accept it and shut up about it. But it does not work that way. Both the toddler and elementary child would require something greater of me … patience and understanding. Simply put, healing takes time.

In order for my sons to heal, I would have to be patient enough to allow the healing process to be complete. Even as adults we do not always get over painful situations quickly. We easily ruminate over the circumstances just as children do in their own way. Patience is a necessity for healing.

Too often when something fails we are quick to point blame. It temporarily reduces the pain and suffering when we can locate a cause. It is equally just as challenging to look within ourselves to take accountability for what is wrong or broken. When raising children, the years are delicate and pass us by so swiftly. In a blink those years are gone and the child has become a young adult. All the blaming, angst, and fretting during or even after a divorce becomes so trivial.

I listened to a young patient of mine openly discuss how sad she was that her divorced parents did not get along. She went further to say every major decision that affects her results in her suffering because the co-parents are still blaming each other for what went wrong in the marriage and they have been divorced over ten years now. The co-parents attempt to punish each other by withholding cooperation, but in the end, she admitted to being the one that is hurt. She desired a certain cosmetic treatment that was costly and would have meant the world to her esteem. The patient concluded that the years drug on without a single treatment being rendered because the parents kept the pain going long after the divorce was final.

It is not easy by any means as I reflect on my own misfortune through divorce. But healing through the pain certainly is doable. I invite you to think on three practices to pursue:

- Assign responsibility appropriately
- When in need don't wimp out on seeking Therapy

- Always apply Intuitive thinking in order to receive the healing that is necessary to raise children appropriately during this distressing transition

Assigning responsibility appropriately lends us the opportunity to utilize what was discussed in the previous chapters. It is without a doubt that tempers are quick to flare during divorce. Just the slightest of offenses can set one if not both parties off. It was so in my case. Just when calmness would seem visible, out of nowhere a phone call from the attorney or another bill in the mail or another challenge for custody with another court date would rear its ugly face. This would trigger all the emotions and sometimes it occurred in the presence of children. Like it or not, they are watching.

Finger pointing comes and we don't want to be wrong in front of the children. As a parent, I never want to let my children down, let alone be the cause of their pain and suffering. But I found that just taking accountability for what I was responsible for made the healing a lot easier. Even further, apologizing for the role I played would certainly go a long way.

My ex-husband and I were in the kitchen with my sons sitting at the breakfast bar eating, all the while listening in on our conversation. He and I were discussing the sale of the home mingled with me attempting to reach an agreement to keep the home. He casually emoted that if it were not for me causing the divorce I would not have to be in the position to bargain to keep the home. In that moment, I could feel the heat rising just beneath my collar deep into my flesh. But, my sons were watching and listening. They were looking and listening to see if I would apply that lesson I so etched in their minds via a poem by Rudyard Kipling. "If you can keep your head when all about you are losing theirs and blaming it on you." I had made it a necessity that they memorized that poem, especially being males. Within every verse this powerful poem provides the guidance and the path to becoming a man, just as the poem's ending declares. So, I entered a state of mindful awareness and compassion for my soon-to-be ex and responded accordingly.

You are correct, I am to blame for the dissolution of the marriage but only partly. I am to blame because I entered willingly into this marriage where I was still broken from the first marriage. I offered you a fractured woman who could not receive nor give what was needed for the marriage to survive. And now it leads me to a position to advocate on behalf of the children to surrender to some resolution to keep the home. I further stated that despite what percentage of the responsibility I can assume, it would not do any good for me to begin calculating where the remainder of the blame should fall. The home fell into the hands of a realtor who placed it on the market. But this moment would not be my defining moment of my deepest truth. I cannot hide the nature of my pain over the loss of the family home. The pain that already entered and saturated my heart and mind like a toxic gas was now taking root and spewing other emotions. In a conversation with a relative, who patiently listened as I ranted about the loss of my first purchased home, there was the truth surfacing. My regret in that instant was that I lacked the power to be faster than sound. For if I had possessed such ability, I would have snatched back those four words before she heard them.

The words spoken would lead to a deep moment of veracity that would expose the true source of my pain.

From my lips the four words burst through as I gasped trying to inhale them back. "I hate being married." My relative said, "Aha, there it is." She was right. Truth and blame reared its face beneath all the pain and loss. Upon her inquiry as to why I "hated being married," I answered with a clear assignment of blame that I viewed marriage as a thief that robbed me of my voice, my identity, leaving me without a clue as to who I was. The next question she asked me was profound, evoking self-analysis. "Did marriage take your voice and identity, or did you give it away?"

My truth revealed in its entirety would lend a deeper understanding that the loss of the home was not the root of my pain. Upon discovery of my truth and assigning the responsibility I played in the downfall of my marriage, I could more easily accept the consequences of divorce. One consequence was the loss of the family home.

I had accepted my responsibility. Once that occurs finding fault in someone else is pointless. The compassion I would continue to show my ex-husband despite many olive branches returned to me that were broken would soften everyone's resolve and healing would be able to penetrate. This in no way is to be interpreted that guilt should be a companion to anyone during the healing process. There is a marked difference between guilt and accountability. Guilt during a divorce is absolutely pointless. Life happens and it is not always good. Life contains within its realm beginnings and endings. The ending of a marriage with children does not dictate how the children evolve. For I have witnessed multiple accounts where a two-parent household yields damaged and broken children/adults just as easily as a single parent household.

While guilt implies bad or wrongdoing, accountability is taking ownership of one's actions. By being accountable, I was able to heal rather than taking on guilt that the marriage did not work. I was able to help my children to a pathway of healing through this pragmatic approach. I would explain to them that life does not always operate perfectly. There will be hardships, disappointments, and sadness just as there is happiness, success, and good fortune. In explaining this to my sons one day, they reflected on that very poem I encouraged them to commit to memory. Is it like the poem says, if you can meet with Triumph and Disaster and treat those two impostors just the same…? I smiled knowing that they were getting it. They were healing through the pain, this great mediator of life bridging life experiences with the lessons of life. It is not enough to just throw blame, take accountability for what you can and let go of the rest. The children will take a silent yet deep appreciation for this.

The children can hold guilt beyond measure. It is reasonable to expect the children to internalize suffering because they make up one half of the person being discarded as a soulmate via the divorce. When disgust is felt about a behavior trait of the co-parent, the children can easily hold themselves with fault and blame the tension in the home on themselves. I would pay careful attention to this by praising them in all their God given attributes. I would often remind them how fortunate I was to have carried and birthed them. As a reminder, I would never end these moments of praise without stating that I willingly had them and I willingly chose their father because of such fine characteristics he possessed. I would list them and identify those characteristics in them.

We must always project truth. We entered into the marriage with complete autonomy. No one forced us.

It was not a prearranged marriage. I would stand before my sons with complete accountability that I chose this marriage with your father as I chose to have you. As part of healing, I relied heavily upon table talk with my sons. I would say: Please forgive my disapproval of him at this moment because I am cross with sadness, disappointment, and anger. However, as you may be cross with me one day over grounding you, does that mean that my goodness and value as your mother is diminished?

We try as parents to be omnipotent when raising and rescuing our children. But, there are some things that are too heavy to hold. Divorce, careers, raising children, finances, etc. all being juggled at the same time can be too much to handle. It can take some people to a breaking point. This is the place where you have to submit and ask for help.

Frankly, I was forced into group therapy sessions. It was mandatory in my region that divorce couples with children attend a required number of these group sessions. My pompous attitude about it all was, "I don't need to be told how to be a good parent because I already am a phenomenal parent." I gritted my teeth and seethed the entire fifteen-minute drive to this meeting place. I had to sign-in, wear a name badge and sit amongst seventy-five people to receive lectures like I was back in undergraduate lecture halls. I took my seat in the very back of the lecture room next to the door. My mind was stiff with refusal and resentment at this mandate. Needless to say, my resistance would soften with every class as I watched, listened, and learned about behaviors that would arise and circumstances that would challenge me beyond my expectations. Now I never did change my seating position, but my mind and heart were open and resulted in receiving a wealth of information that would benefit my children.

Therapy is nothing to feel intimidated about. We all need help at some point in our lives. Some children will have a hard time coping with so many transitions hitting them at once. In my children's case, within a year's time span they had watched their home being sold, their dog being sent to a shelter, resided in multiple residences as we moved from one rental to another. And yet they were still expected to perform well in school and activities. For children, pressure like that can create cracks in the seams. Therapy can be medicine for the mind, body, and soul.

Intuitive thinking is a process that will serve as a useful navigator through the healing process. I employed this many, many times over. I love how Albert Einstein viewed intuitive thinking as he is quoted saying, "The intuitive mind is a sacred gift and the rational mind is a faithful servant. We have created a society that honors the servant and has forgotten the gift." Everything is not black or white, there are so many more layers with varying shades and hues in between.

My ex-husband made a statement that would only be spat from the rational mind. He would often say that because of the divorce I had chosen to be a part-time mom. Well, rationally speaking, yes, I will have part-time custody of my children. But I knew that I could not explain the intuitive reasoning for me being a full-time mom. Instead, I would have to show it. It is a painful reminder of what divorce costs as I settled into a new home and half of that time was spent with my children in another home. However, the reality is I am no part-time mom. I would present this to my children on a constant basis that I am one hundred percent a mother as you cannot sift through the biological connection and sever it in any portion. It cannot be dissected in any manner. For instance, my son chose to play the trumpet in his school band. I watched him struggle with the lessons and fingering. I purchased a trumpet on eBay for myself. The nights that he spent at his father's house, I studied the fingering on YouTube, practiced his scales, made copies of his band lessons, and learned them. When he would return to my house, in awe, he would stand with his trumpet as I would invite him to play with me and we would push each other together. He became quite skilled and soon surpassed me. While I no longer am able to hang with him, I have since placed him with a private instructor. Now, I could have lamented over not having my children, I could have even fought in courts over having primary custody, but the intuitive mind knew that I could be a parent one hundred percent of the time and not have them in my presence. I did this with book reports as I would read them too. I would grocery shop with them in mind so as to have their favorites prepared when they arrived. Or I would have gotten all the materials they needed to move forward on specific academic projects. My sons had not learned to ride a bike before the divorce. On my days/nights without them, I would study YouTube for techniques to teach them. This helped with healing because I did not consume myself with the angst. In the time it would take for the rational mind to think on the tragedy of not having my children full-time or wondering what they were doing with their dad and comparing or finding blame, the intuitive mind would be busier conjuring ways to seamlessly bridge the gaps between the fractures.

On this bridge that I was strategically building and reinforcing, I would throw in one more component that made it strong as steel. My communication would have to be not only confident but so open that it hardly seemed like a gap at all. I knew I was successful in this bridge building campaign when my sons would ask whose weekend is it, yours or Dad's. I had the internal pat on the back moment. For I had made the gap between the homes so smooth, they would forget just as I and my ex would at times as to whose weekend it was with our sons.

My communication was open always, never closing for one instant. We maintain a shared email account alongside our private accounts. This way all school information is sent to one email and we can see it. Every bit of information that comes home from the children's backpack that involves parent involvement I snap a photo and send it to him. My home is structured so that if my sons need their father for any reason he is welcomed. Even if they want challenge him in a PlayStation game, they have the autonomy to call their father and set time for him to come over to play. It was critically important for me to maintain a state of visibility. Being visible and present as parents ties into the basic and fundamental need of every young child. It is the need to experience a sense of predictability and safety. When your child's daily routines become disrupted and unpredictable (e.g., who picks them up from school, who wakes them for school in the morning, or even how long before they see the other parent) it challenges their ability to feel safe and secure.

My ex-husband and I were given certain days with our children, but I never once played into that judicial game. I was very exact in my manner that under no circumstances would either parent be considered a non-parent because it was a Tuesday vs. Wednesday. I was very emphatic that I am a mother every day just as he is a father every day. I would maintain as much consistency as possible to provide the security my children needed. If my ex took our sons to the barbershop on Wednesday, despite Wednesday being my designated day to pick up my children from school, I would invite him to continue to pick up our sons and take them to the barber. Just as he always picked them up from school, I encouraged that practice, so they would never guess as to who is picking them up. Small tokens of visibility and presence of the parent aided in healing. After all, I wanted to a be a cure for my children not the disease.

I cannot stress to you enough through my experience how the presence of each coparent is essential to the lives of children you are raising during this critical period. While coparenting, never underestimate the power of communication. Partnering and planning to support the children mandates that communication must flow openly with the children as well as between households for the gaps to be smoother. Not all gaps will close as it is still part of the many fractures that exist with divorce. My suggestion is to close the gaps that can be sealed and the others…. Well use them as a teachable moment for life. While I was not going to change my household rule on bedtime for the sake of sealing a gap, I did use it as a teachable moment. These very gaps and fractures we experience during divorce, whether they are rules, distance, or even absence by a co-parent, are all part of life during the divorce process. All of these painful experiences are a part of life that can occur at any stage. I thought it to be prudent to have my sons face them front and center as life and not as some cruel fate of theirs solely because they were products of divorce.

BRIDGING THE GAPS

I would admittedly acknowledge that the largest gap of all is the divided household. Open communication was and still is a beautiful bridge between the gaps. I fought hard to build a sturdy bridge and this part of the process is no matter to take lightly. The greatest conquests are harmony and uniformity. I would prey upon my creative thinking and pray to my God that I could just get right because my sons' mental, emotional, psychological well-being hinged upon me getting it right.

Just the mere fact that two separate homes weigh heavier on the pockets adds tension. Money is always at the center of tension and arguments when it is off-balance. Two homes mean two of everything. Needless to say, this did not sit well with my ex. He would understandably grumble and it would make tensions rise to the point my sons would wear it on their faces. In one instance my ex-husband had called me asking, "Where are their jeans that I bought? They were wearing those brand-new jeans when they went to your house." My initial mental reaction was, "Oh no, not that baby mama got the clothes and won't give them up crap. Here we go." My sons were next to me listening as his vexed tone in his voice escaped the phone. They again were watching me. I responded with what size were the jeans and where did you purchase them. He proceeded to make me aware of how slack of a mother I was because I had not a clue as to what size jeans they were wearing. I took ownership of that since I did not buy the clothes during the marriage, as I lack any sense of fashion, and so I never checked for the sizes. I ended the conversation with, I will fairly make things right. My sons admitted that they disliked the tension and it seemed to be over something petty, articles of clothing. I asked them where does dad buy your jeans. Upon them telling me, I took them to the store to pick out the very jeans he had purchased and had them try them on. The next day, I handed him two pairs of jeans for each pair that went missing. I had even purchased additional pairs of jeans for my home. This way the only jeans they would wear back and forth would be the brand that he selected. My solution was that I was able to guarantee my ex a pair of jeans that matched what he bought. After all, he was the one that dressed them during the marriage. About six months later, I found those jeans in one of their bins. I called him up and apologized that I had those jeans. We laughed over the fact that they had outgrown those jeans now. And I said, exactly why I don't fuss over those things. Life is short and whatever I can do within reason to bridge the gap I will do for the sake of their childhood.

Another hurdle that can seem insurmountable is house rules. Especially since divorce yields two houses. I realized that I could in no way take on the mindset that his house was not a part of me nor vice versa. While there are two households, the children are still one body and I had to maintain that awareness. To bridge the two households is a daunting task when the judgements are flying at an all-time high. The children will naturally compare everything. From the rules, the bedtime, the chores, and even the discipline. I remember a family member who went through the same process years before me complaining that the children were pitting her against the ex. But, as I stood on that path, I saw it differently. It is a simple compare and contrast that occurs naturally with human beings. For the children, a juvenile mindset, it is expected that this desire to compare will occur. The transition is hard enough, now there are two different lifestyles accompanied by two different lifestyle languages that they are quickly thrust into learning for their survival. Some children get it quickly, others do not. With those statistics regarding children of divorce still lurking in my conscious, I felt it imperative that I bridge this gap swiftly and as accurately as possible.

I knew this scenario was coming. I had viewed the previews of the divided house from others before me as they suffered through their separation and divorce while raising children. One Sunday morning my sons began to challenge me about their bedtimes and why Dad made them go to bed earlier than I do. They began to grumble that he never makes allowances if they are in the middle of their show and want to finish it. For he is indeed a stickler for the 8:30 p.m. bedtime. No ifs, ands, or buts were allowed with him. As for me, I would bend a little, well a lot more than he. I would allow up to 9:15 p.m., which is a lot of time in a child's point of view. They didn't stop there, they further challenged why did I press them on academics the way I did. "Dad said the report looked nice, why do I have to rewrite it?" With this dynamic of conflict, I assessed that their grasp on two different set of rules was slippery. I did not perceive it as they were attempting to pit one parent against the other. They were understandably trying to make sense of it. And of course, they would lean to the rule that presented its best favor for them. On the way to church, I met with their verbal challenges in this way. I expressed that the two different rules existed even as we existed in one household because Dad and I are two people with two different views. The marriage did not change our views, but the one household encouraged us to seek compromise. Now that we are in two different households we do not have to make such compromises as before. Then my youngest son chimed in that he likes my house better because of the bedtime rules. My response I gave was so clear without complication that I never had another issue about rules between houses again. I said to them, "Do you get to watch your iPad on Saturday morning at my house?" "Yes," they replied. "Are you watching your iPad this morning?" "No, of course not. We can't watch videos in church while the pastor is preaching, that is disrespectful to God!" I further examined them by asking if they would like to speak with the pastor to complain that the rules of the Lord's house differs from their mother's house. They remarked how silly that seemed. My final question to them, "Since you love watching videos early in the morning at my house, would you say that my house is better than the Lord's house?" Without hesitation they ejected the answer "No!" They had concluded that every house has different rules whether it be the school house, Lord's house, my house, or Dad's house. Those rules would inevitably require respect and obedience. It is an understanding that I pressed upon them at this major gap in their lives that is simple to bridge. No one exists within just one structure. Our lives are constantly moving, and we transition through many places that come with their own set of rules. I chose with a mindful awareness and intuitive thinking not to burden my children with thinking that the only time you will encounter such contrast in life is through the divorce. If I had done that, it would have deposited something toxic in them. They may have viewed every transition that requires an adjustment to rules and guidelines as negative instead of necessity to succeed. I further explained to them that rules will change between teachers as they move upward academically and are assigned to multiple teachers in a school year. Rules are what they are in different facilities. These varieties in rules don't just appear because you are in different households. They are a part of life. My sons just received the lesson and adapted early.

REBUILDING A NEW LIFE

I quickly will attest to the fact that rebuilding can oftentimes feel more challenging than the divorce itself. It was as if life left me with scraps and dared me to rebuild this new life even better with those measly snaps from wreckage. With my children as motivation, you bet I did just that. I took every single scrap and rebuilt a new life for my children. And oh my God was it one of the greatest challenges of my life that I did not do without some grumbling and complaining. During my childhood, when I would complain about tough times, my mom would kindly recite a quote by John Milton. "The mind is its own place and in itself, can make a heaven of hell, or a hell of heaven." These words would weigh heavy on my tired mind and heart as I embarked on the reconstruction of life for my children and myself.

As with all darkness, the light is bound to shine through. The dust will settle as the divorce comes to an end, yielding some resolution. Children are gifted a strong sense of resilience through their youthful innocence. As adults, we embody the power that will encourage their growth in resilience, mindfulness, and compassion among other attributes to succeed in life. As we move on beyond the divorce, the children will remain our priority as we continue to raise them through the milestones of their development.

I have since made it through the darkest hours of separation and divorce while raising my children. Now in separate homes my ex-husband and I raise our children together with a like-mindedness. Our communication and sharing of responsibilities are stronger than ever. Oftentimes I will remark to a family member or friend that the co-parenting is better now than during the marriage. So much to be said for irony. We not only raise the children effortlessly now, but we continue to work together. Rebuilding the new life for the children is easier than you think when you make it through the previous stages and remain intact. Keeping the long-term vision very clear will enable a smoother transition through divorce. Despite the back and forth visits to court and the extreme demands coupled with accusations, I held my children close to heart for motivation to see me through the trying times. I trusted my visions for the future that if I exercised the points of M.O.T.I.V.A.T.I.O.N. things may not become perfect, but they will definitely be better for all involved.

Long-term vision in raising my children with a co-parent did not include being stuck in chaos. I envisioned exactly where we are now. I would often speak that to my ex-husband as we navigated those murky waters of separation and divorce. I would blatantly admit that I needed him to raise the children. I refuse to be consumed by the negative emotions that tag along with the process because I was afraid I would deposit that into the children. I expressed to my ex-husband that the case with all the in-depth legal issues was heavy, but I understood he was hurting. To further patiently understand his anguish, I began to view his temperamental reactions the way I would with my three-year-old. Sometimes, you have to allow the frustration to run its course before you can get through to the ill-tempered individual. And so it was with my situation. Our divorce extended three years non-stop to the point it had two separate case numbers. But here we are with a new life and new foundations set for the children.

My greatest moment of elation is having table talk with my sons and their pointing out to me that they are the strongest mentally and emotionally, and can take on a lot in life because of how we handled the divorce.

With rebuilding, work is never done with regard to raising children. New challenges will arise that test you. The obstacles can seem even greater after the divorce as each person settles into their new lives and new routines. Children begin to transform and their perspectives shift, as do ours as parents. A new life can even mean more distance between the parents as careers grow and change bringing about distance in living locations.

What happens when these pitfalls occur at the conclusion of the divorce and you are trying to remain motivated as you once were in the thick of things? I invite you to take the time to think upon several points I introduce in the next chapter as W.A.T.E.R.

CONQUERING PITFALLS

In my process of divorce with my sons front and center, I pulled from an invaluable resource to keep me focused and on track. With a long-term vision as to where I saw myself and my children, I pulled from the elements of W.A.T.E.R. Every living specimen requires water. We need this every day in one form or another.

Wait. I often would find myself with so many wounds of divorce –whether they were financial, emotional, or mental–were devastating. When we first experience pain on any level, it is the natural survival instinct to fight or take flight. It is equally just as easy to make rash decisions just to find temporary relief. Short-term vision cheats everyone. Instead focusing on long-term goals and solutions yields positive long-term gains when strategies are thought out carefully when rebuilding.

Some decisions just require you to be still for a moment. Some conversations require holding your tongue. This is a sensitive time for the children as they are watching and listening when we least suspect. Every action on our behalf are small deposits made within the children. If we are quick to anger and react it is understandable that the children will ingest these negative emotions and actions. However, if the reverse occurs, children will learn how to healthily react during stressful situations. It mattered to me what I was depositing into my sons. For I was certain that my expectations of a positive withdrawal would be expected from me. I would still require good behavior in school accompanying excellent grades. I would expect them to settle respectfully into a new life and have patience as the journey would be long and bumpy.

Waiting can be trying. But just taking a breath or two before taking any actions can prove to be resourceful. I often imagine where would I be right now if I had expressed anger to every major offense during the divorce. What state would my children be in? Would I really still have my co-parent by my side working with me professionally and personally as we watch our sons thrive into their teenage years and on to adulthood. I cringe to think of how toxic life would be if I had not stood still, taking a breath and counting to ten before acting quickly out of anger.

Analyze. I recall in grade school being asked to grade my own paper following a quiz. It's a self-challenge to mark your own paper, especially when being wrong. It causes a sort of reflection that shines a light on imperfections. It is much easier to just not look into that mirror. There was a time when my oldest son expressed he wanted to join the competitive summer swim team. He was twelve. He had never swam competitively before. Furthermore, he had never done a competitive dive nor a could he even complete a turn in the water. One day he went to practice the dive and found that all he could do was belly flop because of his fear of diving head first into the pool. I was restless with him after many attempts. As he stood on the edge of the pool with his courage soaked in hesitation, I blurted, "Just belly flop into the pool." His face showed his annoyance with the false encouragement and responded with, "That is not the correct way to dive, I can't simply dive like that at a meet." We soon left the center to head home. I broke the silence with an interpretation as to why I made such a request. It is too often that we are afraid to dive in because we are grading ourselves constantly. We want to move from a grade F to a grade A++ in an instant. We know that we are not prepared for the A so we stand there never moving at all because we are stuck at F. Stuck in Fear which results in failure. I said to him, if you had done the belly flop it moves you from an F to a D. D=Doing something. You will be so surprised of how quickly you can rise to the A or even an A+ zone once you move from an F zone to the D zone. The next practice, he dove in head first but with a knee bent. He climbed out of the water exclaiming, "Yes! I am out of the F zone." Within that week he would dive head first without even a knee bent. I just winked and said the A is coming.

I share that because I felt the angst of not always knowing the right thing to do or say to my children. Every child is unique with their own set of needs. It is easy to feel like I was failing because they were being pulled through so much negativity. I would stop and grade my own paper and see that every time I listened to them, shared with them, spoke patiently and encouraged a good rapport with their father, I was moving from F to A+ raising them through this difficult time.

Thankfulness. It is so hard to be grateful when the life is breaking off in pieces around you. I remember the first time my sons asked, "Where do we find the positive thing in all of this when we are sad or angry?" They further questioned how could I find any happiness going back and forth to court with a tug-of-war over them. I answered them in truth that while it is not easy, there is always something to be grateful for even in the least of life. I expressed that while the divorce case is lengthier, and cost more than I would ask for, I was thankful that God had provided me the means to fight for them. Just as so it was with the divorce itself. The marriage may not have worked out, but it yielded me two beautiful children.

I would take the point of thankfulness one step further with my sons to drive the message home. One day a commercial for Saint Jude Children's Research Hospital appeared on the television as my sons and I watched. My youngest son asked me to explain the reason for donating to Saint Jude. I opened up a YouTube video to show both my sons patients of Saint Jude. I explained to them that life breaks for everyone, no one is spared despite their status, their upbringing or their faith. I turned to both of them and asked, "If you could choose your breaking point in life would it be living in two separate households or the fate of the young boy in Saint Jude?" They responded quickly, "We would accept the divorce and two separate households." I nodded, precisely my point. Life will break, but remember the breaks can always be worse than what they are. No matter the trials, there is always someone less fortunate.

Expectation. Knowing what I wanted and why was key to moving from one phase of the divorce to the next while raising children. I would have to obtain a high degree of clarity as to what I wanted and expected of myself and of my children. It obviously will help in the legal realm. But, even more so with the children. At the onset of my separation, a telephone conversation with a friend made me squirm while I stammered through a tough question. He asked, "What is it that you want?" It seemed such a simple question. I would be faced with that question from my attorney, family, and friends alike.

In order to make it through the process, I needed to keep the transition simple. The legalities of the divorce were already a strain. I began to list my expectations, ensuring they were realistic. Simply, I wanted a safe place for my children and I wanted to be the best parent I could be. This short list would prevent me from being overwhelmed. If I included expectations on the list that involved me altering my ex-husband's disposition, or his involvement that would lead to more negative reactions and outcomes.

In the beginning of the separation after the sale of the family home, I remember developing high levels of anxiety because I stressed myself with thoughts, vexed about how to regain another home. One day I relayed to my sons that it may be a while before we have another home. They responded that as long as we were together, safe, and happy they could wait as long as it takes for another home. I saw then that the short list of expectations, as long as the list was practical, was all I needed. This reduced my tension and anxiety significantly.

Release. As the famous Christian quote goes, at some point you just have to "let go and let God." It is what it is. Just like that glass dish I mentioned in an earlier chapter that fell with both sons responsible, you have to sweep up the pieces, place it in its respective place and move forward. Again, it is what it is. It is a divorce. Ok, you had to sell the home. But just as I learned the one-bedroom apartment can be just as much of a home as the two-car garage three-level luxury home.

Release is a process of freeing yourself of what you cannot control. Hold to what is important. The moments with the children, the conversations, the laughter, the good times. Because in the midst of the trials there is good, there is always good. Be mindful of the things you hold onto because the greatest moments that are happening to you will slip by you and the regrets will be all you will end up with. Hold on tight to what matters most and for the rest, just let it go.

CONCLUSION

The divorce process is truly a harrowing experience. The sadness, pain, and anger that come along with it are so huge that it overwhelms you and could cause you to lose control of yourself. It can disorganize you and leave you almost useless and powerless. The countless hours you spend in the court, the quarrels that seem like they're never going to end can be blinding to what is important in life and everything else that is good. You can imagine how much of your life you're wasting by fighting your partner over who is wrong or right and who should acquire which assets.

To simply sum it all up: put the children first. Within that simple statement, I acknowledge there is so much complexity. Oftentimes I wished for some device to give me a quantitative result on just how well I was parenting through divorce. Was I making progress at getting the single parent thing right or was I completely failing my children were questions I constantly pondered. Yes, the statistics and society's standards constantly inject doubt every step of the way.

I found my own barometer for success. Just as heavily as I relied on the resource of M.O.T.I.V.A.T.I.O.N. to be the best parent I could be during and after divorce, I relied on the feedback from my children as the measure of my success. Children are extremely keen and when given a safe space they will communicate very effectively what they are feeling. It is through exercising all the techniques through M.O.T.I.V.A.T.I.O.N. I could assess just how progressive my sons were in transitioning through the stages of divorce.

My greatest discovery was in obliging my eldest son's request to select a book for his first book report as he started sixth grade. To me it was a big deal. His entering the preteen phase and asking for my help was a big deal to me. I was more than overjoyed to select the book. As I stated, I do practically everything with my children with the M.O.T.I.V.A.T.I.O.N. method.

I knew I could not squander this opportunity, this chance to connect with my son. With a mindful heart I carefully considered exactly what I wanted him to read, which I knew he would remember for a lifetime. My selection was the book by Chinua Achebe *Things Fall Apart*. I needed a book that would allow us to talk, allow me to listen. This would be a platform where he could be in his zone, the academic, and just feel free and safe to discuss as he pleased.

My son took hold of the book and naturally questioned why this book. I answered him that this book stood out to me because it had been gifted to me over twenty-five years ago by a dear friend when I needed it the most. I read this book again as my son read it. After he finished the book, I received much more than what I intended.

We engaged in a dialogue about the characters. What he had extracted from the book stunned us both. I asked him which character stood out the most and why. My youngest son, quite intrigued, listened on. My eldest son stated that the main character weighed heavy on him from the first chapter to the last.

It was in this carefully meditated selection of a book, just a book, where a moment of veracity would rear its head again for me. My son claimed that the character was hurt from childhood and carried it throughout his adult life. He went on to address that in spite of all the disappointment in this character's childhood, he managed to excel but yet not live a fulfilling life.

"Aha, yes son," I replied excitedly. I was employing an intuitive mind to oblige my son's request at selecting a book for a book report. This exercise would, in turn, be a dose of therapy through communication. "Now I want to ask one final question that is not posed as a requirement to your book report ... but first list the literary conflicts you discovered in this book." He listed all the ones that appealed to him. "For my final question, what is the conflict that grabs you the most?" He first answered quickly "Man vs. Man," but just as quickly as he answered he retracted the response.

I would have easily settled for that conflict, but his next response left me spellbound. He said, "I take that back. The conflict that really grabbed me was Man vs. Himself." I could not even get the question of why out before my youngest son asked, "What does he do to himself?" My oldest answered intuitively, because of the character's childhood and where he grew up he could never express himself. It was forbidden. So, he carried with him all the pain and suffering into his adult life. Despite the fact that he was highly respected in his community, and had the favor of strength and wisdom, he would succumb to his own demise.

I nodded with much respect that I had just received my grade as a parent. I was headed in the right direction. I summed it up for the both of them that life will break, it will fall apart. If you don't address the infirmities that cause the breaks they will haunt you. You must embrace the pain. You must communicate effectively to heal. I expressed to both my sons, although I love all your accomplishments, despite all the honor rolls, awards, and trophies you bring home if you are not healed from any of life's breaking moments the war you fight within yourself will undo all you have accomplished.

My youngest was eager to weigh in on the summation of the book. He remarked that when he gets married and has children he will have them read it too. It wasn't so much about the book anymore as it was about his statement. Despite my failure at marriage, both sons still see themselves married with children in the future. I asked them both, you would still want to marry even after the three years of witnessing the devastation of divorce and all its losses. My youngest said, "Yes Mom, because that was your failure and you taught us to write our own life story."

The fears that first crept upon me in the hotel room that first night of separation were softened in that moment. The therapy was more for me at this moment than for my sons. I cringed every moment of the divorce process, frightened that they would be permanently scarred in some way. I feared that as they would live in split homes, it would damage them beyond repair. But I basked in knowing my M.O.T.I.V.A.T.I.O.N. plan was working. It would take just love and compassion. My ex-husband would show up as I needed and desired to be a wonderful co-parent. My sons' pain and all the emotions that tagged along would enter a state of healing, and they would thrive and see life just as it is. It is what you make of it.

Single parenthood is not easy by any means. Divorce, should you choose that path with children, will render very dark moments. I pray the children will be the source of motivation for your strength to get through the difficult times, where you can help them heal with you.

I conclude this with one final token. I reflect on a conversation I held with my father after the birth of my oldest son. You see, I was fretting over private schools and how I wanted him to be schooled, raised, etc. My father patiently looked at me and said, "Remember you are merely a foster parent. He is not your son for he belongs to God. You have been merely granted the favor of temporary custody over his life. It is your job to raise this child to be equipped to fulfill the destiny that God has already planned." Both my sons were motivation for me to remember the favor bestowed upon me. That is to be the best mother I could be. I would express my gratitude whether going through a devastating divorce or after by being focused on building them up rather deconstructing them to be pawns used as weapons for retaliation. Don't sweat the small stuff. Only change what you are in control of and release the rest.

ACKNOWLEDGMENTS

My gratitude runs infinitely deep to many wonderful people enabling me to give birth to this book. This book was merely a concept, just an idea in my head. I thank God for placing the right people on my path who encouraged, motivated, and prayed for me.

I am extremely grateful for my parents instilling within me life lessons providing me the strength to always pursue my dreams and never stopping until I have made them a reality.

To my sister: I have the utmost love for you always believing in me even in my moments of doubt. My brother, how I love your pragmatic approach to life and I have carried pieces of your advice with me in life.

To my sons: I am grateful for being granted the opportunity to be a mother to you both.

You have changed my life in every way, challenging me to be a better person every day.

To DeWayne, my best friend: I appreciate you and your support despite the hurdles we have had to jump. But we landed just fine.

To the Morgan James Publishing team: Special thanks to David Hancock, CEO & Founder for believing in me and my message. To my Author Relations Manager, Tiffany Gibson, thanks for making the process seamless and easy. Many more thanks to everyone else, but especially Jim Howard, Bethany Marshall, and Nickcole Watkins.

And never could I close without thanking Dr. Angela Lauria and her team for pressing and shaping me into the author I was created to be. I am blessed to have created a book that will be a blessing to many others.

About the Author

Tanzania Davis-Black is an immensely passionate dentist. Born and raised in Lumberton, NC, she earned a B.S. in Dental Hygiene from The University of North Carolina at Chapel Hill. Inspired to pursue her childhood dream of becoming a dentist, she enrolled at Howard University College of Dentistry. She acquired a Doctor of Dental Surgery degree (DDS) and successfully completed her residency at Howard University Advanced General Dentistry program.

In 2002, Dr. Davis-Black founded a private dental practice in Bowie, Maryland. Over the years she has received significant acclaim and recognition for her work. She is an active member of several professional organizations such as Academy of Cosmetic Dentistry, Academy of Implant Dentistry and Academy of General Dentistry. An advocate for community service, Dr. Davis-Black is always eager for an opportunity to volunteer. She is also a member of the Dental Honor Society, Omicron Kappa Upsilon.

In her spare time, Dr. Davis-Black loves to spend time with her family, especially her two sons. She actively participates in sports and music and has a love for reading and writing. Currently residing in Maryland, Dr. Davis-Black's primary objective is to change the smiles of the community one patient at time. She serves with an aim to inspire and motivate others to live their best lives.

Additional Resources

To receive an additional resource to accompany the book *When Life Breaks: Raising Children During Divorce* please visit www.whenlifebreaks.com. Upon entering your initials and email address a copy of the e-workbook will be forwarded to your email.